Genealogical Sources
for Marriage Officiants
of Baldwin County, Alabama
1866 - 1910

"Family Worship in a Plantation in South Carolina." *Courtesy of the New York Public Library, Digital Collections.*

by

Carolyn E. Hood-Kourdache

©2016

Printed in the U.S.A.

"And Do You ... Take This Man?"

------ Reverend Jefferson Ellis, Pastor
      Bethel Baptist Church
      Montrose,
      Baldwin County, Alabama
           1867

by

Carolyn E. Hood-Kourdache

©2016

Printed in the U.S.A.

"And Do You ... Take This Man?"

------ Reverend Jefferson Ellis, Pastor
       Bethel Baptist Church
       Montrose,
       Baldwin County, Alabama
          1867

Contents

Acknowledgments

I respectfully acknowledge the Schomburg Center for Research in Black Culture, Photographs and Prints Division, The New York Public Library. in the online Digital Collections, for the illustrations in this book. To my family and friends, thank you.

Illustrations

Cover
Schomburg Center for Research in Black Culture,
Photographs   and Prints Division, The New York   Public
*Library. **"Family worship in a plantation in South Carolina"***
New York Public Library Digital Collections. Accessed June 7,
2016.   http://digitalcollections.nypl.org/items/b1dd3bd3-
ae7e-dc5d-   e040-e00a1806309d

ii   ***Frontispiece***
Schomburg Center for Research in Black Culture,
Photographs   and Prints Division, The New York   Public
*Library. **"Family worship in a plantation in South Carolina"***
New York Public Library Digital Collections. Accessed June 7,
2016.   http://digitalcollections.nypl.org/items/b1dd3bd3-
ae7e-dc5d-   e040-e00a1806309d

10   ***Emancipation Proclamation.*** *Schomburg Center for Research*
in Black Culture, Photographs and Prints Division, The New
York Public Library. "Proclamation of Emancipation by the
President of the United States Abraham Lincoln." New York
Public Library Digital Collections. Accessed June 10, 2016.
http://digitalcollections.nypl.org/items/510d47df-c211-a3d9-
e040-e00a18064a99

64   *Schomburg Center for Research in Black Culture,*
Manuscripts,   Archives and Rare Books Division,   The New
*York Public Library. **"Black Church."** New York Public*
Library Digital Collections. Accessed June 6, 2016.
http://digitalcollections.nypl.org/items/510d47da-   73c9-a3d9-
e040-e00a18064a99

Preface

Reconstructing the life of one man, Reverend Jefferson Ellis, led to the examination of the lives of his peers. The spiritual, emotional, educational, and political leaders of their congregations, before, during, and after the Civil War, and residents of Baldwin County, Alabama, are delineated within these pages.

These men promoted enfranchisement in Reconstruction-era Alabama. From the pulpit, they encouraged their flocks of freedmen and freedwomen to exercise their civil liberties, by engaging in contracts, such as for labor and marriage. Through marriage, Newly freed women asserted, their personal dominance over their bodies; newly freed men, asserted their humanity and position as stakeholders in the family unit.

Over 800 marriage licenses between 1866 and 1891, were examined. Newly licensed parties sought solemnization of their marriages at the Courthouse, a parent's house, a church, or at the river's edge. Ministers of the gospel, like Reverend Ellis, officiated.

Baldwin County, the oldest county in the state, incorporated in 1809, was the home of the largest nonwhite community, outside Mobile. Enumerated persons of color surged from 1,760, in 1870, to 4,893, by 1880.

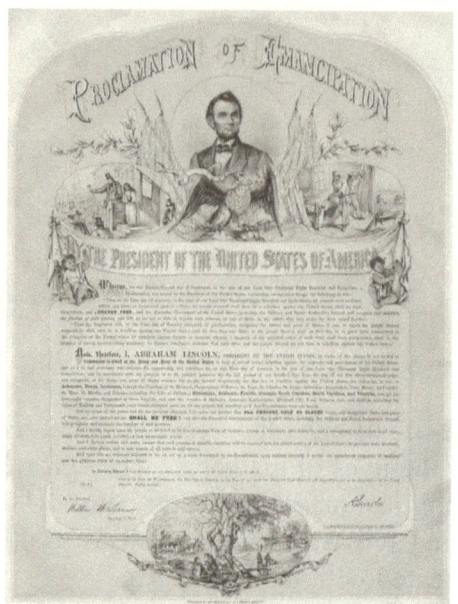

"Emancipation Proclamation."
Courtesy of the New York Public
Library, Digital Collections.

Timeline

1865   Freedmen's Bureau created by Federal
Government

May 30,
1865   Major General Oliver Otis Howard appointed
Commissioner Freedmen's Bureau, issued orders to assistant
commissioners to solemnize former   slave marriages[1]

Sept 8,

1

Reginald Washington, "Sealing the Sacred Bonds of Holy Matrimony
Freedmen's Bureau Marriage Records," *Prologue Magazine*, National Archives
and Records Administration, Vol. 37, No. 1. (Spring 2005),
http://www.archives.gov/publications/prologue/2005/spring/freedman-marriage-
recs.html (accessed: March 2014.

1865 *Alabama's assistant commissioner issued order for "separate record books" for freedmen's marriage licenses[2]*
Probate judges ordered to suspend marriage bonds and reduce marriage license fees[3]

Sept 29,
1865 *Alabama legalized former slave unions, legitimizing their children[4]*

1866 *Baldwin County, Alabama, created separate marriage license book for "newly freed persons of color," as directed[5]*

1867 *Jefferson Ellis, Minister of the Gospel, performed his first recorded marriage solemnization.*

---

2 Ibid.
3 Ibid.
4 Ibid.
5 Alabama County Marriages, 1809-1950.

*Two lovers, hand in hand, in the noonday sun, trod
dreamily down to the river bank. A purposeful visit to
the Fish River, trout wasn't on their minds. No, this
was the start of a shared memory - their wedding day.
Many times in their hearts they stole away. But, now
the joy, Oh the joy to be wed! And, they had a real
preacher coming to bless their union. And it was so
very sweet, the smell of persimmons and honeysuckle.
Wild jasmine and gardenias lined their nuptial path
while birds rang out their chimes. It was a glorious
day!*

Among the many men elected to officiate at the thousands of
wedding ceremonies, was the Right Honorable Reverend Jefferson
Ellis, Pastor, and founding father, of *[Little]* Bethel Baptist Church, at
Montrose and Daphne, Baldwin County, Alabama. Jeffrey Ellis was
born 1821, in Baldwin County, Alabama, a free person of color, and

died there, November 10, 1890.[6][7]

Jeffrey Ellis married Louisa Ann Fecklin *[Ficklin]*, circa 1855, in
Baldwin County, Alabama. He worked as a turpentine hand, while
pursuing his other occupations of teacher, and preacher. He and his
wife had nine children before 1880.[8] Rev. Ellis' brother, Anthony
Ellis, and brother-in-law, George Ficklin were the founding fathers of
the sister/rival church, Macedonia Missionary Baptist Church, in
Daphne, Alabama. Rev. Jeffrey Ellis was not mentioned in the
founding fathers' roster.[9] It is unknown whether he was ever invited to
preach from Macedonia's pulpit. But it is likely that he did so. His
parents were Lowry and Maria Ellis of Baldwin County, as they were
neighbors to another Ficklin. Francis Ficklin was the daughter of
Thomas Ficklin, Jr. and the niece of Louisa Ficklin, Jeffrey Ellis's first

---

6   "United States Census, 1870," index and images, *FamilySearch*
    (https://familysearch.org/pal:/MM9.1.1/MHK4-D6Z : accessed 09 Mar 2014),
    Jeffrey Ellis, Alabama, United States; citing p. , family 34, NARA microfilm
    publication M593, FHL microfilm 000545500.
7   Baldwin County AlArchives Deaths.....Death Index 1886-1894 .
    http://www.usgwarchives.net/copyright.htm (accessed: March 2014).
8   Ibid.
9   Macedonia Missionary Baptist Church. http://www.macedoniabaptistchurch-
    daphne.com/aboutus.html.

wife.[10]

Francis J. Ficklin was Thomas Fickling, Jr.'s daughter.[11] Francis J. Ficklin married John W. Gentry, in 1860.[12] Six years later, Mrs. Fannie Gentry married Henry J. Smith, at Baldwin County.[13] She was last enumerated in Sumter County, in 1880.[14] Francis [Ficklin] Smith died before 1900, in Sumter County, Alabama.[15] Her husband, Henry Smith died in 1913, Sumter County.[16] Ben H.[enry] J. Smith lived in the household of Margaret [Mrs. Smith] McDowell, in 1860.[17] Presumably, Margaret McDowell was his mother. McDowell and daughter Susan, were witnesses on Smith's marriage certificate.[18]

---

10 "United States Census, 1850," index and images, *FamilySearch* (https://familysearch.org/pal:/MM9.1.1/MHP5-34P : accessed 4 March 2015), Francis J Fickling in household of Thos Fickling, Baldwin county, Baldwin, Alabama, United States; citing family 66, NARA microfilm publication M432 (Washington, D.C.: National Archives and Records Administration, n.d.).

11 "United States Census, 1850," : accessed 3 March 2015), Francis J Fickling in household of Thos Fickling, Baldwin county, Baldwin, Alabama, United States; citing family 66, NARA microfilm publication M432 (Washington, D.C.: National Archives and Records Administration, n.d.).

12 "Alabama, County Marriages, 1809-1950," John W Gentry and Frances J Ficklin, 24 Nov 1860; citing Baldwin, Alabama, United States, county courthouses, Alabama; FHL microfilm 1,839,621.

13 "Alabama, County Marriages, 1809-1950," Henry J Smith and Fannie Gentry, 18 Aug 1866; citing Baldwin, Alabama, United States, county courthouses, Alabama; FHL microfilm 1,839,621.

14 "United States Census, 1880," index and images, *FamilySearch* (https://familysearch.org/pal:/MM9.1.1/M4VX-FXY : accessed 3 March 2015), Francis Smith in household of Henry Smith, Brewersville, Sumter, Alabama, United States; citing enumeration district 165, sheet 452C, NARA microfilm publication T9 (Washington D.C.: National Archives and Records Administration, n.d.), roll 0032; FHL microfilm 1,254,032.

15 "United States Census, 1900," index and images, *FamilySearch* (https://familysearch.org/pal:/MM9.1.1/M96M-BM5 : accessed 4 March 2015), Henry Smith, Precinct 10 Bluffport, Sumter, Alabama, United States; citing sheet 8B, family 155, NARA microfilm publication T623 (Washington, D.C.: National Archives and Records Administration, n.d.); FHL microfilm 1,240,040

16 "Alabama Deaths and Burials, 1881-1952," index, *FamilySearch* (https://familysearch.org/pal:/MM9.1.1/F3BM-NPL : accessed 4 March 2015), Henry Smith, 19 May 1913; citing reference p 280; FHL microfilm 1,703,923.

17 "United States Census, 1850," index and images, *FamilySearch* (https://familysearch.org/pal:/MM9.1.1/MHP5-35C : accessed 4 March 2015), Ben H J Smith in household of John Mcdowell, Baldwin county, Baldwin, Alabama, United States; citing family 150, NARA microfilm publication M432 (Washington, D.C.: National Archives and Records Administration, n.d.).

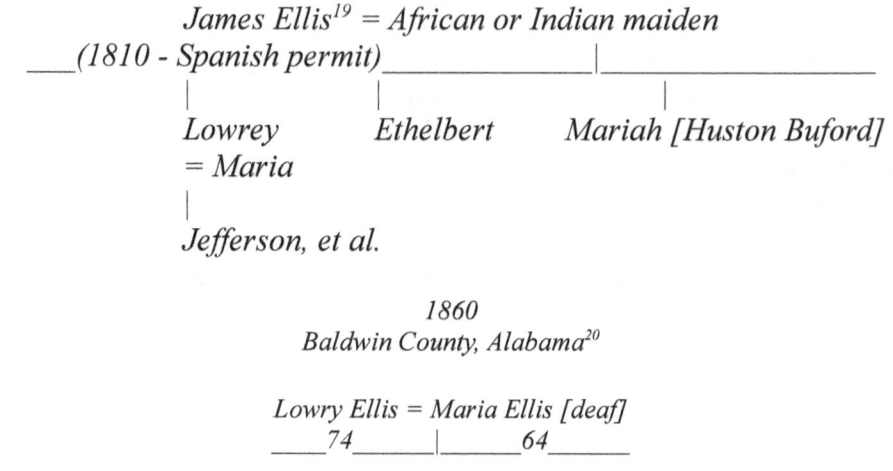

James Ellis[19] = African or Indian maiden
___*(1810 - Spanish permit)*_____|_____

| | |
Lowrey   *Ethelbert*   *Mariah [Huston Buford]*
= Maria
|
Jefferson, et al.

1860
Baldwin County, Alabama[20]

Lowry Ellis = Maria Ellis [deaf]
____*74*_____|_____*64*_____

Francis Ficklin[g] (15 Female)

immediate neighbor in McGill household

An election riot occurred in Baldwin County, in March, 1869.[21] A "radical mob" could not be controlled by local law enforcement. In an effort to maintain racial harmony, Rev. Ellis chaired a meeting of local leaders and clergymen, at the nearby Colored *[African]* Methodist Church, at Montrose, Baldwin County, September 4, 1869.[22] Reverend Ellis was a recognized leader in his community and valued as such after the Civil War.[18] C.S. Lasell was appointed Secretary for the meeting. Lasell departed the area prior to the 1870 enumeration. The meeting was attended by "a few white men of the neighborhood." Copies of the proceedings were forwarded to local newspapers.[19]

This episode was indicative of Rev. Ellis' role as peacemaker, spokesperson, and political activist. Rev. Ellis was instrumental in saving lives, both black and white, during those troublesome months and years, following the Civil War. Rev. Ellis was one of many ministers that enabled the work of the Northwestern Freedman's Aid Society.[20] As fellow religious men, their cooperation was sought.

---

18 Ibid.
19 Ibid.
20 *Letter of the Secretary of War, communicating, in compliance with a resolution of the Senate of December 17, 1866, reports of the assistant commissioners of freedmen, and a synopsis of laws respecting persons of color in the late slave states. January 3, 1867. -- Read and referred to the Committee on Military*

The "societies" and "agencies" left Alabama, after only three or five years. Rev. Ellis was in attendance at a District Baptist Convention. He was noted in an article for such, in 1869, in Selma Alabama.[21] Reverend Ellis believed in civic participation as evidenced by his voter registration in 1867.

Affairs and the Militia. January 21, 1867. -- Ordered to be printed. Date: Monday, January 21, 1867 Publication: Serial Set Vol. No.1276; Report: S.Exec.Doc. 6; Page 6. Source: GenealogyBank.com (accessed: March 2014).
21 Ibid., "Radical Pow-Wow At Selma, First Day of the District Convention" (accessed : March 2014).

Table 1. 1867 Voter Registrants for
Baldwin County, Alabama

Name	Race	Precinct	District
Ellis, Anthony	**African-American**	**5**	**3**
Ellis, Charles	*African-American*	*9*	*3*
Ellis, Charles	*African-American*	*9*	*3*
Ellis, Green	*African-American*	*6*	*3*
Ellis, Jefferson	**African-American**	**5**	**3**
Ellis, Lemuel	**African-American**	**5**	**3**
Ellis, Robert	**African-American**	**5**	**3**
Ellison, Stephen	*African-American*	*4*	*3*

From the Voter Registrants table, we note Reverend Jeffrey Ellis and his brothers Anthony, Lemuel and Robert. Noting the inhabitants of Precinct 5, District 3, that registered to vote on the same day as Rev. Ellis, we learn that of the 270 registrants for the same district, 204 were described as "colored," later "African-American." "Colored" was a more accurate term, as many in Baldwin County, were proximate descendants of the Five Tribes (Cherokee, Choctaw, Chickasaw, Creek and Seminole), that were deported under the Removal Act of 1830.

Building upon Elizabeth Shown-Mills' "association principle," the church most associated with early marriage licenses, and Rev. Jeffrey Ellis, was Bethel Baptist Church, at Montrose/Daphne.[23] The church was established in 1867 by four former slaves with Jeffrey Ellis, as their pastor. The two-acre lot was donated by former slaveholder, Major Lewis Starke. Lewis Starke was a grandson of Margaret Tate, widow of David Tate. The Tates were a prominent family with a long-standing history of slavery in Baldwin County. One of the church trustees, Stamford Starke aka Stanford Sterling was likely Lewis Starke's son, hence the donation. Sterling also had a two-acre lot with house as part of his assets. He did not own land according to the Bureau of Land Management.[24]

A literate man, Rev. Ellis worked in the turpentine industry, one of the harshest in Alabama.[25] It was not unusual for preachers of the era to maintain their "day job." After all, he had nine children to support.

Jefferson Ellis, Minister of the Gospel

Pastor, Founding Father of Bethel Baptist Church

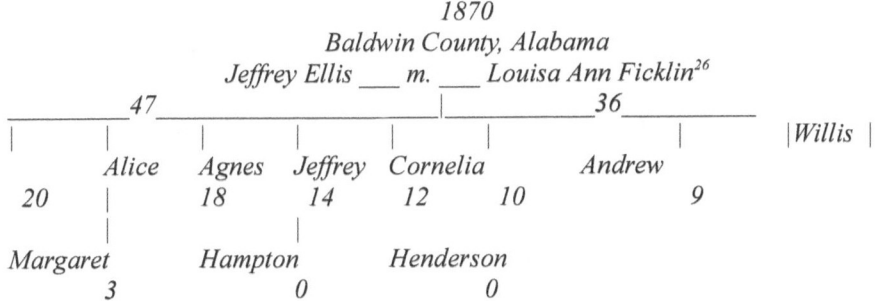

```
                              1870
                      Baldwin County, Alabama
              Jeffrey Ellis ___ m. ___ Louisa Ann Ficklin²⁶
_____47_____|_____36_____
 |      |       |        |         |        |             |       | Willis |
      Alice  Agnes   Jeffrey   Cornelia          Andrew
 20     |     18       14       12      10                9
 |            |
Margaret    Hampton            Henderson
   3           0                   0
```

Jeffrey Ellis, Senior, married Edna Lyons, November 6, 1876, in Baldwin County. Judge Gasgue officiated.[27] Edna Lyons, born in 1816, was enumerated in 1870, with her family, (the Mike Lions household) Baldwin County.[28] Four years later, in 1880, Jeffrey Ellis, twice widowed continued his ministry. He resided in the household of his son-in-law, William Bayley *[Bailey]*, and daughter, Cornelia.[29]

His first wife, Louisa Ann Ficklin, died between 1870 and 1876. Jeffrey Ellis wed Lizzie White, at Daphne, Baldwin County, in 1880; Rev. A. A. Williams officiated.[30] Four years later, in 1884, Reverend Ellis married widow, (and Edna Lyons likely niece), [Francis] Fannie Gardner, in Baldwin County.[31] Judge William H. Gasgue officiated, at his office. The two men were well acquainted and shared a mutual respect. Widow Gardner rose in status as the wife of a prestigious preacher - the Rev. Ellis, Pastor of Bethel Baptist Church. But in six short years, he would be of the ages.

Rev. Ellis' death was a proximate result of ministering to the sick and infirm. The year 1890, was yet another in the successive blights of yellow fever, in Mobile, Alabama, and its outlying areas. His demise, in November, 1890, followed by one month, the institution of the Reed Yellow Fever Commission, at Fort Morgan.[32] Rev. Ellis' burial site is unknown. Perhaps he was buried in the cemetery at Bethel Baptist Church, or within the town of Ellisville, seven miles east of Daphne. If he were a victim of yellow fever, however, his body may not have been buried at all, but consumed in flames.

Genealogical Sources

1880
Baldwin County, Alabama

Jeffrey Elles [Ellis]
|
William Bayley [Bailey] ____ *m.*___ *Cornelia Ellis Bayley [Bailey]*
____24_____|_____19_____
| |
Sarah   *Caroline*

Exhibit 1. Rev. Ellis' First Certification

State of Alabama   )
Baldwin County   )

                                To the Judge of
Probate of said County,
I hereby certify that I joined in the Bonds of Matrimony,
Edward Harvey and Pernelia Baptist, on the 7th day of
September, 1867, at Montrose in said County.

                                Jefferson
Ellis

                                Pastor of
                                [Little]

Bethel Baptist Church[33]

This certification came after "freed persons of color" sought marriage services at the Courthouse. Initially, Judge of Probate Charles W. Wilkins, was assisted by Adolph Feist, Justice of the Peace, and George M. Bonner, J.P., B.C. (Justice of the Peace of Baldwin County), until Bonner died in 1867. Also, lending a Bible were John Wilson, J.P., B.C. and John J. Grace, M.G. The Probate office, overwhelmed, provided a separate license record book in 1866, specifically for the newly "freed persons of color."

Table 2. Some Couples Married by Reverend Jeffrey Ellis
Between 1867 and 1890

Groom	Bride	Date
Benjamin Stallsworth	Rosetta Bonner	October 24, 1869
Allen Revus	Katie Brown	July 5, 1868
George Parker	Eliza McCall	July 6, 1868
Washington Evans	Cora Elwa	November 15, 1868
Andrew Fields	Dina Sibley	April 16, 1870
John Lewis	[sic] Davis	Jun3 15, 1870
Robert Wilson	Ida Harris	Nov 10, 1882,[34]
Charles Camper	Fannie [Francis] Ellis *his niece*[23]	September 24, 1881,[22]
Handy Johnson	Rosetta Lyman	July 13, 1881
Joseph Griffin	Maria Hollinger	June 11, 1881
Frank Reed	Millie Ficklin *his wife's niece*	March 3, 1881,
Isaac Sterrit	Missouri Ely	October 14, 1871
William H. Jones	Flora Williams	September 4, 1871
Giles Edwards	Ellen Tuff	November 7, 1870
Monroe Jordan	Mary Austin	November 3, 1870
James Douglas	Jenny Pleasance	July 27, 1870
Scipio Bailey	Salina Sicily	January 8, 1870
Howard Williams	Josephine Moore	June 21, 1880
McDuffy Loyd	Lucy Ann Randolph	November 22, 1869
Joseph Douglas	Susan McKay [McGillivray not McElroy]	January 16, 1875 at N. [Norman] Durant's,
Willis Hunter	Liddia King	May 11, 1869

---

22 "United States Census, 1880," : accessed 09 Mar 2014), Chas. Camper in household of Jos. Grist, Sibleys Mills, Baldwin, Alabama, United States; citing sheet 182D, family 2, NARA microfilm publication T9-0001

23 "United States Census, 1870,": accessed 10 Mar 2014), Francis Ellis in household of Charles Ellis, Alabama, United States; citing p. , family 17, NARA microfilm publication M593, FHL microfilm 000545500.

Genealogical Sources

Groom	Bride	Date
Anthony Ellis	Narcissa Mitchell	October 31, 1874,
his brother[35]		
Wm. Jack	Eliza Sizemore	May 30, 1874, at Church
Mose Davis	Phillis Ellis	November 2, 1871, his sister-in-law
Ned Taylor	Fanny Davis	November 2, 1871

Reverend Jeffrey Ellis' Family Members

On July 1, 1867, Rev. Ellis and his brothers, Anthony, Robert, and Lemuel Ellis registered to vote for the first time. They were required to swear an oath of allegiance to the United States.[36]

Rev. Ellis was a free person of color, prior to Emancipation in 1860. Jefferson Ellis worked as a laborer in the household of George W. Tucker, Bibb County, Alabama, in 1860. Ellis was born in Alabama, in 1824.[37] Rev. Ellis' association with free persons of color, such as his wife, Louisa Ann Ficklin, and her brother, George Ficklin, provided a clue. Rev. Ellis' ordination date and location were undetermined. The slave "Jefferson" of Petition 21285102, of North Carolina, was discounted. They were distinct persons.[38]

His brother, Lemuel Ellis, resided in Mobile, with his family, by the 1870 enumeration.[39] Robert Ellis was not found further in the record. Robert Ellis' widow, Phillis *[sic]* married Mose Davis, in Baldwin County, in 1871, with Rev. Ellis as officiant.[24] His son, Robert Ellis, purchased land, in Baldwin County, in 1901.[40] Reverend Ellis appears to have been the only ordained minister in his family. No record was found associating Rev. Ellis with military service.

When Rev. Ellis' daughter, Agnes married Wellington Stendley *[Stanley]* (Rev. Hayward Stanleys' son?), in 1874, in Baldwin County, Judge William H. Gasgue, officiated at the Baptist Church.[41] An Agnes Stanley resided as a boarder in the 1880 enumeration, in Selma, Dallas County, Alabama, as a single, white female, or passe blanche.[42] Willis Ellis, was not enumerated in the State of Alabama, for the 1880 Census. Daughter, Alice Ellis married James Henry Brown, at the Courthouse.[43] Alice Brown married Oliver Dumas, three years later, in 1874.[44] Judge Gasgue officiated. Alice Dumas believed her father to be a native son of Virginia, and her mother was born in Alabama.[45] Son, Jeffrey Ellis married Lizzie White, at Daphne, Alabama. Rev. A. A. Williams officiated.[46] Daughter, Cornelia Ellis, married William *[Winslow Bailey]*, at her father's house. Rev. Ed. Jackson officiated.[47]

---

24 "Alabama, County Marriages, 1809-1950," : accessed 26 Mar 2014), Moses Davis and Phillis Ellis, 02 Nov 1871; citing Baldwin County; FHL microfilm 1839621.

And son, Andrew Ellis, married Ellen Gardner, in Judge Gasgue's office, Judge Gasgue officiated.[48] Andrew Ellis died in 1928, in Daphne, Alabama.[25] Cornelia Ellis Bailey, died in 1930.[49]

Henderson Ellis, a twin son, appeared on a marriage document for John Hurley Ellis, in 1944, father of the groom.[50] The other twin, Hamilton, appeared on a marriage document in Mobile. As his given age is 28, he is 10 years too young to be the son of Rev. Ellis, but was possibly his grandson.[51]

Yet another son, Jeffrey *[T.J.]* Ellis, born 1856, in Massachusetts[?], enumerated in 1880, as a school teacher and next-door neighbor to Rev. Ellis.[52] T.J. Ellis married Priscilla Webster, in Baldwin County, in 1877.[53] Priscilla Webster Ellis was Ellen Gardner Ellis' cousin. Priscilla's son, Rev. Ellis' grandson, Thomas Ellis married, in 1897, at Mobile, to Mary Williams.[54]

> *What God hath joined together*
> *Let no man put asunder.*
> *Amen.*
>
> *I now present to you*
> *Mr. and Mrs....*

---

25 "Alabama, Deaths, 1908-1974," Andrew Ellis, 28 Mar 1928; citing reference cn 5193, Department of Health, Montgomery; FHL microfilm 1908451.

Hayward Stanley, M.G. and Minister M.E. Church
1816 - before 1924

Minister, Hayward *[Haywood]* Stanley, born in 1816, in North Carolina, resided in Township 6, Baldwin County, for the 1870 enumeration.[55] Haywood Stanley married Jane Denton, May 8, 1870, in Baldwin County.[26] Rev. Virgil Burke (Zion Chapel), officiated. Jane Denton was not his first wife. He was a 53-year-old carpenter, and lived with his wife, Jane, and his two children, Ferdinand and Dorasker.[27] By the 1880 census, Stanley lived in Tatemville [David Tate's former property], with his wife Jane, and niece, Arabella Denton.[28] Rev. Stanley's grandson, Haywood Kirkman, died in 1939, in Baldwin County.[29] His daughter, Dora Stanley Kirkman, died in 1952, at Fairhope, in Baldwin County.[30] His wife, Jane, died at Fairhope, in 1924.[31] She was a widow.[32]

Rev. Stanley could neither read but nor write; hence, his "mark," on marriage records. It is doubtful that any of his sermons survive for that reason.

1870
Baldwin County, Alabama

Hayward Stanley ____ *m.* ___ *Jane Denton Stanley*
_____53__|_____40_____
 | |

---

26 "Alabama, County Marriages, 1809-1950," : accessed 15 Mar 2014), Hayward Stanley and Jane Denton, 08 May 1870; citing Baldwin County; FHL microfilm 1839621.

27 Ibid.

28 "United States Census, 1880",: accessed 12 Mar 2014), Haywood Stanerly, 1880.

29 "Alabama, Deaths, 1908-1974," : accessed 12 Mar 2014), Dora Stanley in entry for Haywood Kirkman, 27 Jul 1939; citing reference cn 14161, Department of Health, Montgomery; FHL microfilm 1908578.

30 "Alabama, Deaths, 1908-1974," : accessed 12 Mar 2014), Dora Kirkman, 25 Jan 1952; citing reference 21, Department of Health, Montgomery; FHL microfilm 1908866.

31 "Alabama, Deaths, 1908-1974," : accessed 12 Mar 2014), Hayworth Stanley in entry for Jane Stanley, 16 Feb 1924; citing reference cn 2256, Department of Health, Montgomery; FHL microfilm 1908256.

32 Ibid.

Ferdinand P. Stanley   *Dorasker Stanley*
                    20   *12*

Based on the record, Rev. Stanley was minister of the Colored, now African Methodist Episcopal Church at Montrose, Baldwin County, Alabama.

Table 3. Some Couples Married by Reverend Stanley

1869 - 1870

<u>Groom</u>	<u>Bride</u>	<u>Year</u>	<u>Venue</u>
Davis, John	*Johns, Mary*	*1869*	
Guyon, Alex	*Mills, Sally*	*1869*	
Howard, Alfred	*Liggins, Adeline*	*1869*	
Scott, Dick	*Sunior, Sirah [sic]*	*1869*	*Battles Wharf*
Sanders, Ben	*Evans, Sara*	*1869*	*Battles Wharf*
Jackson, Green [sic]	*Allen, Mary*	*1870*	*Battles Wharf*
Ebon, Silvester	*Thomas, Rose*	*1870*	*Tatemville*
Hill, Benjamin	*Fowler, Lucy C.*	*1870*	*Fish River*
Williams, Giles	*Blake, Francis*	*1870*	*Fish River*
Fisher, Rufus	*Davis, Mattic*	*1870*	*Battles Wharf*
Tarvin, John	*Wade, Becky*	*1870*	*Fish River*
Saunders, Henry	*Washington, Mahaley*	*1870*	*Fish River*
Washington, Peter	*Bettus, Emilina*	*1870*	*Tatemville*

Ephraim Spradley, M.G.

1844 - 1910

Ephraim Spradley *[Spratley]* born 1844, in Alabama, resided with his family, at Montgomery Hill, Baldwin County, Alabama, for the 1870 enumeration.[33] Rev. Spradley married his first recorded couple in 1871. In 1880, he was enumerated as a preacher.[34] His son, E.C. married Maria Mack, in 1890.[35] His daughter Mary, married Thomas Moore, in 1891. Both marriages were solemnized by Rev. John Jacobs.[36] Edward Spradley died at Tensaw, Baldwin County, in 1910.[37] Rev. Spradley purchased 80 acres, in 1883.[38]

1870
Baldwin County, Alabama

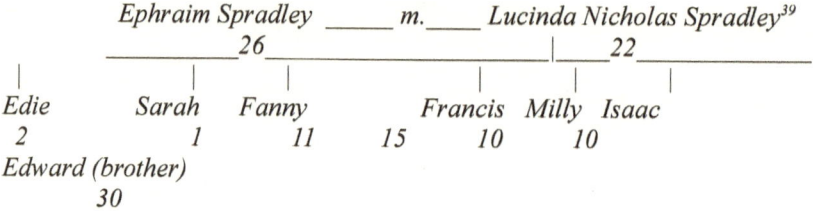

Ephraim Spradley _____ m. ____ Lucinda Nicholas Spradley[39]
26 | 22

Edie   Sarah   Fanny   Francis Milly Isaac
2   1   11   15   10   10
Edward (brother)
30

Rev. Spratley's daughter, Lucinda Williams, died in 1930, in

---

33 "United States Census, 1870", : accessed 12 Mar 2014), Ephraim Spradley, 1870.

34 "United States Census, 1880", : accessed 12 Mar 2014), Ephm Spratley, 1880.

35 "Alabama, County Marriages, 1809-1950," : accessed 12 Mar 2014), E C Spratley and Maria S Mack, 17 Apr 1890; citing Baldwin County; FHL microfilm 1839622.

36 "Alabama, County Marriages, 1809-1950," : accessed 12 Mar 2014), Thomas Moore and Mary E. Spratley, 08 Aug 1891; citing Baldwin County; FHL microfilm 1839622.

37 "Alabama, Deaths, 1908-1974," : accessed 12 Mar 2014), Ephriam Spratley in entry for Edward Spratley, 03 Apr 1910; citing reference cn 241, Department of Health, Montgomery; FHL microfilm 1894073

38 BLM-GLO. http://www.glorecords.blm.gov/results/default.aspx?searchCriteria=type=patent|st=AL|cty=003|ln=spradley|sp=true|sw=true|sadv=false (accessed : March 2014).

39 Ibid.

Mobile.[40] His son, Ed, died, at Tensaw, Baldwin County, in 1910.[41]
Rev. Ephraim Spratley's daughter, Lawenia [Luvenia] Spratley,
married Edmund Bailey, in 1908, Baldwin County. Rev. Will Leggett
officiated. Nearly thirty years earlier, Will Leggett, was Rev. Spratley's
neighbor.[42]

---

40 "Alabama, Deaths, 1908-1974," : accessed 15 Mar 2014), Ephraim Spradley in
     entry for Lizzie Williams, 27 Jun 1930; citing reference cn 14750, Department of
     Health, Montgomery; FHL microfilm 1908479.
41 "Alabama, Deaths, 1908-1974," : accessed 15 Mar 2014), Epram Spradley in
     entry for Ed Spradley, 03 Apr 1910; citing reference cn 242, Department of
     Health, Montgomery; FHL microfilm 1894073.
42 Year: *1880*; Census Place: Montgomery Hill, Baldwin, Alabama, ED : 001;
     Description: Montgomery Hill : Ancestry.com (accessed: March 2014).

John Jacobs, M.G.
1846 - 1926

Reverend John Jacobs was born in 1846, in North Carolina. He worked in the turpentine industry at the 1870 enumeration.[43] Rev. Jacobs resided with his wife Kizzy [*Keziah*] and daughter, Nelly A., in Baldwin County, in 1870.[44] Rev. Jacobs applied for a marriage license with Keziah (unknown), in 1872.[45] Rev. Jacobs applied for a marriage license with Anna Covy, in 1892, in Baldwin County.[46] Reverend John Jacobs died in 1926, at Mount Vernon, Mobile, Alabama.[47]

1870
Baldwin County, Alabama

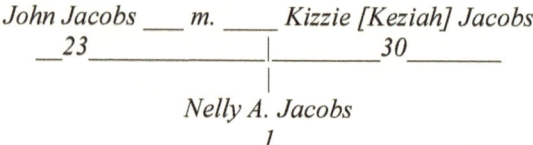

John Jacobs ___ m. ____ Kizzie [Keziah] Jacobs
__23_____|_____30_____
|
Nelly A. Jacobs
1

Reverend Jacobs bought land in Baldwin County, in 1904 and 1906.[48]

---

43 "United States Census, 1870," : accessed 18 Mar 2014), John Jacobs, Alabama, United States; citing p. 10, family 86, NARA microfilm publication M593, FHL microfilm 000545500

44 Ibid.

45 "Alabama, County Marriages, 1809-1950," : accessed 18 Mar 2014), John Jacobs and Keziah, 20 Apr 1872; citing Baldwin County; FHL microfilm 1839621.

46 "Alabama, County Marriages, 1809-1950," : accessed 18 Mar 2014), John Jacobs and Anna Covy, 25 Mar 1892; citing Baldwin County; FHL microfilm 1839622.

47 "Alabama, Deaths, 1908-1974," : accessed 18 Mar 2014), John Jacobs, 14 Nov 1926; citing reference cn 26460, Department of Health, Montgomery; FHL microfilm 1908438.

48 Bureau of Land Management, General Land Office Records. (Hence: BLM - GLO). http://www.glorecords.blm.gov/results/default.aspx?searchCriteria=type=patent|st=AL|cty=003|ln=jacobs|fn=john|sp=true|sw=true|sadv=false (accessed: March 2014).

William Singleton, M.G.

1854 - 1933

William Singleton, laborer, was the son of Hannah Singleton, as enumerated in 1880, Baldwin County.[49] Twenty years later, however, Singleton was a preacher and neighbor to Rev. A. A. Williams.[50] Rev. Williams daughter, Elmira, married William Singleton, at Little River, Baldwin County, in 1894. Rev. Adam Brown officiated.[51] Rev. William Singleton died in 1933, in Washington County, Alabama.[52]

1880
Baldwin County, Alabama

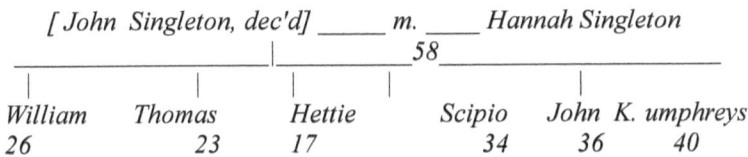

[John Singleton, dec'd] ___ m. ___ *Hannah Singleton*				
_____|_____58_____				
William	*Thomas*	*Hettie*	*Scipio*	*John K. umphreys*
26	*23*	*17*	*34*	*36 40*

Thomas Singleton, M.G.

1857 - 1910

Thomas Singleton, M.G., Rev. William Singleton's younger brother, was born 1855 *[sic]*, in Alabama. He resided with his parents John and Hannah, in Baldwin County, for the 1870 enumeration.[53] In 1900,

---

49 "United States Census, 1880", : accessed 12 Mar 2014), William Singleton in entry for Hannah Singleton, 1880.

50 "United States Census, 1900", index and images, *FamilySearch* (https://familysearch.org/pal:/MM9.1.1/M9ZL-8KT : accessed 12 Mar 2014), William Singleton, 1900.

51 "Alabama, County Marriages, 1809-1950," : accessed 12 Mar 2014), William Singleton and Elmira Williams, 06 Nov 1894; citing Baldwin County; FHL microfilm 1839622.

52 "Alabama, Deaths, 1908-1974,": accessed 12 Mar 2014), Will Singleton, 31 Mar 1933; citing reference cn 6286, Department of Health, Montgomery; FHL microfilm 1908508.

53 "United States Census, 1870," : accessed 12 Mar 2014), Thomas Singleton in

he was still a farm laborer and resided in his mother's house.[54] By 1910, he was an unmarried preacher and resided with his maiden sister.[55] Rev. Thomas Singleton died in 1910, at Tensaw, Baldwin County, Alabama.[56]

household of John Singleton, Alabama, United States; citing p. 10, family 79, NARA microfilm publication M593, FHL microfilm 000545500.

54 "United States Census, 1900," : accessed 12 Mar 2014), Thomas Singleton in household of Hannah Singleton, Precinct 1 Montgomery Hill, Baldwin, Alabama, United States; citing sheet 6A, family 115, NARA microfilm publication T623, FHL microfilm 1240001.

55 "United States Census, 1910," index and images, *FamilySearch* (https://familysearch.org/pal:/MM9.1.1/MK3V-NR4 : accessed 12 Mar 2014), Thomas Singleton, Blacksher, Baldwin, Alabama, United States; citing enumeration district (ED) 1, sheet 11B, family 152, NARA microfilm publication T624, FHL microfilm 1374014.

56 "Alabama, Deaths, 1908-1974," : accessed 12 Mar 2014), Thomas Singleton, 11 Aug 1910; citing reference cn 232, Department of Health, Montgomery; FHL microfilm 1894073.

Alfred A. Williams, M.G.

1857 - 1920

Alfred A. Williams was born December, 1857, in North Carolina. He resided at Montgomery Hill, Baldwin County, with his wife, Viney, for the 1900 enumeration.[57] Widower Rev. Alfred A. Williams married widow Susan Douglas, in 1903, in Baldwin County.[58] Rev. S. B. Bracy officiated. Rev. Alfred A. Williams died in Daphne, Baldwin County, Alabama, in 1920.[59] Rev. A. A. Williams was the pastor of the Macedonia Missionary Baptist Church, in Daphne, Baldwin County, Alabama, in 1879.[60] The Macedonia Missionary Baptist Church, was founded by George Ficklin, William Bailey, Sr., Anthony Ellis, and others, during Reconstruction. We now know that the founding coincided with that of Bethel Baptist Church, earlier in 1867.

1880
Baldwin County, Alabama[61]

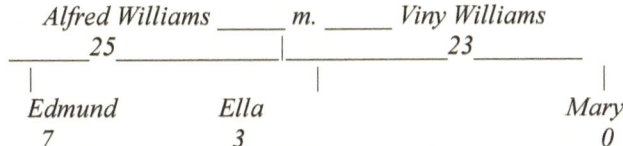

Alfred Williams	m.	Viny Williams
25		23

Edmund	Ella		Mary
7	3		0

Stephen B. Bracy, M.G.

1853 - 1923

---

57 "United States Census, 1900," : accessed 12 Mar 2014), Alfred A Williams, Precinct 1 Montgomery Hill, Baldwin, Alabama, United States; citing sheet 19A, family 392, NARA microfilm publication T623, FHL microfilm 1240001.

58 "Alabama, County Marriages, 1809-1950," : accessed 12 Mar 2014), Alfred A Williams and Susan Douglas, 24 Sep 1903; citing Baldwin County; FHL microfilm 1839624.

59 "Alabama, Deaths, 1908-1974," : accessed 12 Mar 2014), Alfred Williams in entry for Susin Williams, 07 Apr 1920; citing reference cn 7026, Department of Health, Montgomery; FHL microfilm 1908219.

60 Macedonia Missionary Baptist Church.

61 "United States Census, 1880," : accessed 15 Mar 2014), Alfred Williams, Court House, Baldwin, Alabama, United States; citing sheet 194C, NARA microfilm publication T9.

A native son of Alabama, Rev. Stephen B. Bracy, a turpentine worker, resided with his wife Hanna, and young son, Taylor, in Baldwin County, for the 1880 enumeration.[62] Through faith and philanthropy, he adopted three orphans by 1910.[63] Yet another son, Gale Bracy was adopted by 1920.[64] His son, Steve Bracy married Laura Tompkins, in 1908. Rev. Bracy officiated.[65] His son, Israel married Millie Harris, in 1914.[66] Beginning in 1885, Rev. Bracy pastored the Macedonia Missionary Baptist Church, in Daphne, Alabama. His ministry there lasted 38 years. The church was rebuilt under his auspices.[67] Stephen B. Bracy, M.G., died November, 1923, in Baldwin County.[68]

1880
Baldwin County, Alabama

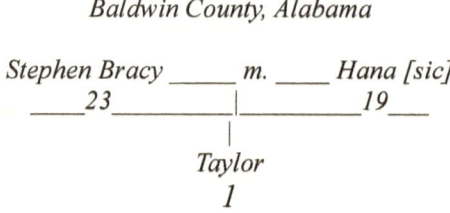

Stephen Bracy _____ *m.* _____ *Hana [sic]*
_____*23*_____|_____*19*___
|
Taylor
1

---

62 "United States Census, 1880," : accessed 12 Mar 2014), Stephen Bracey, Lowells, Baldwin, Alabama, United States; citing sheet 218C, NARA microfilm publication T9.

63 "United States Census, 1910," index and images, *FamilySearch* (https://familysearch.org/pal:/MM9.1.1/MK3V-JH9 : accessed 12 Mar 2014), Steven B Bracy, Stapleton and Ducks, Baldwin, Alabama, United States; citing enumeration district (ED) 7, sheet 2B, family 45, NARA microfilm publication T624, FHL microfilm 1374014.

64 "United States Census, 1920," index and images, *FamilySearch* (https://familysearch.org/pal:/MM9.1.1/MXCG-M3T : accessed 12 Mar 2014), Steven Bracy Sr., Stapleton, Baldwin, Alabama, United States; citing sheet 11B, family 171, NARA microfilm publication T625, FHL microfilm 1820002.

65 "Alabama, County Marriages, 1809-1950," : accessed 12 Mar 2014), Steve Bracy and Laura Tompkins, 19 Nov 1908; citing Baldwin County; FHL microfilm 1839624.

66 "Alabama, County Marriages, 1809-1950," : accessed 12 Mar 2014), Israel Bracy and Millie Harris, 19 Dec 1914; citing Baldwin County; FHL microfilm 1839624.

67 Macedonia Missionary Baptist Church, Daphne, Alabama, About Page. http://www.macedoniabaptistchurch-daphne.com/aboutus.html (accessed: March 2014).

68 "Alabama, Deaths, 1908-1974," index, *FamilySearch* (https://familysearch.org/pal:/MM9.1.1/JDLS-J76 : accessed 12 Mar 2014), S B Bracey, 26 Nov 1923; citing reference cn 22117, Department of Health, Montgomery; FHL microfilm 1908253.

Henry Monday, M. G.

1850 - before 1910

Rev. Henry Monday, was born in Alabama, in 1850 [1856], married Harriet Henderson, in 1872, in Baldwin County.[69] Rev. Spratley officiated. Henry Monday was the next-door neighbor of Rev. Ephraim Spratley, at Montgomery Hill, for the 1880 enumeration.[70] His widow, Harriet Monday, died February, 1928, in Baldwin County.[71]

1880
Baldwin County, Alabama

Henry Monday ___ m. ____ *Harriet Henderson Monday*
_____24_____23_____

Rev. and Mrs. Monday remained childless.

---

69 "Alabama, County Marriages, 1809-1950," : accessed 12 Mar 2014), Henry Monday and Harriet Henderson, 27 Nov 1872; citing Baldwin County; FHL microfilm 1839621.

70 Year: *1880*; Census Place: *Montgomery Hill, Baldwin, Alabama*; Roll: *1*; Family History Film: *1254001*; Page: *152D*; Enumeration District: *001*; Image: *0309*.

71 "Alabama, Deaths and Burials, 1881-1952," : accessed 15 Mar 2014), Harriett Monday, 02 Feb 1928; citing reference 1631; FHL microfilm 2218268.

Lewis Oliver, M.G.

1848 - unknown

Reverend Lewis Oliver, born in Alabama, in 1848, was a laborer on a forced work gang, in Ward 7, Mobile County, Alabama, for the 1870 enumeration.[72] Lewis Oliver, a free person of color, resided with his mother, Jane Oliver, in Mobile, for the 1860 enumeration.[73] He was not found further in the record.

Joshua James, M.G.

1846 - 1918

Joshua James, M.G., was born in 1846, in Alabama, and resided in Monroe County, Alabama, for the 1870 enumeration.[74] Ten years later, he resided in Baldwin County, with his wife, Madora.[75] Rev. James lived with his wife Madora *[Dora]*, and adopted daughter, Suky Green, in Baldwin County, for the 1910 enumeration.[76] Rev. Joshua

---

72 "United States Census, 1870," : accessed 15 Mar 2014), Lewis Oliver in household of Joachim Eslava, Alabama, United States; citing p. 94, family 722, NARA microfilm publication M593, FHL microfilm 000545530.

73 "United States Census, 1860," index, *FamilySearch* (https://familysearch.org/pal:/MM9.1.1/MHDF-KTZ : accessed 19 Mar 2014), Jane Oliver, Sixth Ward City Of Mobile, Mobile, Alabama, United States; citing "1860 U.S. Federal Census - Population," *Fold3.com*; p. 24, household ID 188, NARA microfilm publication M653; FHL microfilm 803017.

74 "United States Census, 1870," : accessed 12 Mar 2014), Joshua James, Alabama, United States; citing p. 192, family 1555, NARA microfilm publication M593, FHL microfilm 000545531.

75 "United States Census, 1880," : accessed 12 Mar 2014), Joshua James, Bay Minette, Baldwin, Alabama, United States; citing sheet 173C, NARA microfilm publication T9.

76 "United States Census, 1910," index and images, *FamilySearch* (https://familysearch.org/pal:/MM9.1.1/MK3V-GDD : accessed 15 Mar 2014), Joshua James, Bay Minette, Baldwin, Alabama, United States; citing enumeration district (ED) 5, sheet 24A, family 507, NARA microfilm publication T624, FHL microfilm 1374014.

James, died at Bay Minette, Baldwin County, Alabama, in 1918.[77] Rev. James purchased land in 1895, Baldwin County.[78]

1870
Monroe County, Alabama

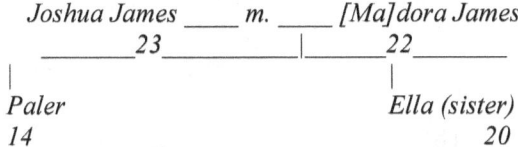

Joshua James _____ m. _____ [Ma]dora James
_____23_____|_____22_____
| |
Paler   *Ella (sister)*
14   *20*

1880
Baldwin County, Alabama

Joshua James ___ m. Madora James

Rev. Logan W. Oldfield

1846 - before 1900

Logan Oldfield married Josephine Henderson, 1867, in Mobile County, Alabama.[79] Born in 1846, in Alabama, Rev. Logan W. Oldfield, resided with his family in Baldwin County, for the 1880 enumeration.[80]

_____

77 "Alabama, Deaths, 1908-1974," : accessed 12 Mar 2014), Joshua James, 19 Mar 1918; citing reference cn 104, Department of Health, Montgomery; FHL microfilm 1908194.

78 BLM-GLO. http://www.glorecords.blm.gov/results/default.aspx? searchCriteria=type=patent|st=AL|cty=003|ln=james|fn=joshua|sp=true|sw=true| sadv=false (accessed : March 2014).

79 "Alabama, Marriages, 1816-1957," Index, FamilySearch (https://familysearch.org/pal:/MM9.1.1/FQKS-RX5 : Accessed 12 Mar 2014), Logan Oldfield and Josephine Henderson, 22 May 1867; Citing Reference ; FHL Microfilm 1294435 V. 1-2.

80 "United States Census, 1880," index and images, *FamilySearch* (https://familysearch.org/pal:/MM9.1.1/M4N1-HVH : accessed 12 Mar 2014), Logan Oldfield, Tatemville, Baldwin, Alabama, United States; citing sheet 201B, NARA microfilm publication T9.

1880
Baldwin County, Alabama

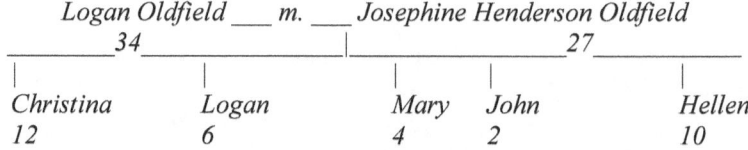

Logan Oldfield ___ m. ___ Josephine Henderson Oldfield

Christina	Logan	Mary	John	Hellen
12	6	4	2	10

Son, Robert, born in 1888, died in Mobile, in 1919.[81, 82] Widow, Josephine, died in 1931, in Mobile, Mobile County.[83] Her birth year was incorrectly stated as 1872. She was married in 1867, ergo, error. Daughter, Hattie *[Helen]*, Sims died in 1943, in Mobile.[84] Hattie *[Helen]* married Albert Sims, in 1908, in Mobile.[85] Daughter, *[Margaret]* Christine Crosby, born 1883, died in 1930, in Mobile.[86] Son, John, married Sadie Easton, in 1901, in Mobile.[87] Finally, Daughter, Clara, married Willie Tunstall, in 1903, at Mobile, Mobile County, Alabama.[88]

---

81 "Alabama, Deaths, 1908-1974," index, *FamilySearch* (https://familysearch.org/pal:/MM9.1.1/JDKT-FBB : accessed 15 Mar 2014), Robert Oldfield, 22 Feb 1919; citing reference cn 250, Department of Health, Montgomery; FHL microfilm 1908211.

82 Ibid.

83 "Alabama, Deaths, 1908-1974," index, *FamilySearch* (https://familysearch.org/pal:/MM9.1.1/JDGL-ZQC : accessed 20 Mar 2014), Josephine L. Oldfield, 13 Sep 1931; citing reference cn 20788, Department of Health, Montgomery; FHL microfilm 1908492.

84 "Alabama, Deaths, 1908-1974," index, *FamilySearch* (https://familysearch.org/pal:/MM9.1.1/JD15-GTM : accessed 20 Mar 2014), Logan Oldfield in entry for Hattie Sims, 08 Jul 1943; citing reference cn 14085, Department of Health, Montgomery; FHL microfilm 1908628.

85 "Alabama, County Marriages, 1809-1950," index and images, *FamilySearch* (https://familysearch.org/pal:/MM9.1.1/VRV4-ZB7 : accessed 20 Mar 2014), Albert Sims and Hattie O Field, 06 Aug 1908; citing Mobile County; FHL microfilm 1550510.

86 "Alabama, Deaths, 1908-1974," index, *FamilySearch* (https://familysearch.org/pal:/MM9.1.1/JDGS-3G6 : accessed 20 Mar 2014), L. W. Oldfield in entry for Margarett Christine Crosby, 30 Jun 1930; citing reference cn 14754, Department of Health, Montgomery; FHL microfilm 1908479.

87 "Alabama, County Marriages, 1809-1950," index and images, *FamilySearch* (https://familysearch.org/pal:/MM9.1.1/VRV4-9GW : accessed 20 Mar 2014), Jno J Oldfield and Sadie Easton, 30 Apr 1901; citing Mobile County; FHL microfilm 1550507.

88 "Alabama, County Marriages, 1809-1950," index and images, *FamilySearch* (https://familysearch.org/pal:/MM9.1.1/VRV4-QGM : accessed 20 Mar 2014),

William M. Mason, M.G.
1810 - before 1900

William. M. Mason was born in 1810 in Alabama, and resided with his wife, Ellen, Ward 6, Mobile County, Alabama, for the 1870 enumeration.[89] Rev. Mason voted in 1867, Mobile County.[90] William Mason, a cotton sampler, married Eliza Raspus, in 1874, in Mobile County.[91] They were enumerated as a family in 1880, in Mobile County.[92]

Willie Tunstall and Clara Oldfield, 15 Dec 1903; citing Mobile County; FHL microfilm 1550508.

89 "United States Census, 1870," index and images, *FamilySearch* (https://familysearch.org/pal:/MM9.1.1/MHKG-SVQ : accessed 19 Mar 2014), Wm Mason, Alabama, United States; citing p. 62, family 520, NARA microfilm publication M593, FHL microfilm 000545530.

90 Alabama Department of Archives and History, ADAH. http://www.archives.alabama.gov/voterreg/results.cfm (accessed: March 2014).

91 "Alabama, Marriages, 1816-1957," index, *FamilySearch* (https://familysearch.org/pal:/MM9.1.1/FQKM-KVW : accessed 19 Mar 2014), William Mason and Eliza Raspus, 05 Jan 1874; citing reference ; FHL microfilm 1294437 V. 4-5.

92 "United States Census, 1880," index and images, *FamilySearch* (https://familysearch.org/pal:/MM9.1.1/M4VQ-3J5 : accessed 19 Mar 2014), William Mason, Mobile, Mobile, Alabama, United States; citing sheet 258B, NARA microfilm publication T9.

Table 8. 1867 Voter Registrants for

Mobile County, Alabama

Name	Race	Precinct	District
Mason, Frank	African-American	7	1
Mason, Harry	African-American	7	1
Mason, John	White	5	2
Mason, Leonard	African-American	7	1
Mason, Lewis	African-American	1	2
Mason, Richard	African-American	7	1
Mason, Simon	African-American	5	2
Mason, Theo	African-American	1	1
Mason, Wm M	**African-American**	**7**	**1**

1880
Mobile County, Alabama

```
William Mason ___ m. ___ Eliza Raspus Mason
_____70_____35_____|
          |              |              |
Samuel  Raspus    Willie Raspus   William Raspus
         9              14              13
```

Twice a widower, Rev. Mason married Harriet Powell, in 1876, in Mobile County.[93] Their son, William Walter Mason, died in 1915, in

93 "Alabama, Marriages, 1816-1957," index, *FamilySearch*
    (https://familysearch.org/pal:/MM9.1.1/FQKM-KJV : accessed 19 Mar 2014),

Mobile County.[94] Rev. Wm. Mason died before 1900, because he was not found further in the record.

William Mason and Harriet Powell, 08 Jul 1876; citing reference ; FHL microfilm 1294427 V. 25-27.

94 "Alabama, Deaths, 1908-1974," index, *FamilySearch* (https://familysearch.org/pal:/MM9.1.1/JKQH-6YW : accessed 19 Mar 2014), William Walter Mason, 06 Sep 1915; citing reference cn 572, Department of Health, Montgomery; FHL microfilm 1894121.

William D. Mayo, M.G.

1822 - before 1900

William D. Mayo, was possibly a free person of color, born in 1822, in Virginia, and had sufficient income to hire two servants for the 1880 enumeration, in Baldwin County, Alabama.[95] He resided at Montgomery Hill, with his wife, Hannah. Rev. William D. Mayo purchased land in 1896, in Baldwin County.[96]

1880
Baldwin County, Alabama

William D. Mayo _____ *m.* ___ *Hannah Mayo*
_____*58*_____*65*_____

Adam Brown, M.G.

1835 - before 1930

Adam Brown married Eliza Sims, May 15, 1875, Rev. Ephraim Spratley officiated, in Baldwin County.[97] Adam Brown wed Miss Nora Williams, 18th December, 1884, Baldwin County, Alabama, Rev. A. A. Williams, officiated.[98] The venue was St. Joseph's Church. Adam

---

95 "United States Census, 1880," index and images, *FamilySearch* (https://familysearch.org/pal:/MM9.1.1/M4N1-QTN : accessed 12 Mar 2014), Wm Mayo, Montgomery Hill, Baldwin, Alabama, United States; citing sheet 140C, NARA microfilm publication T9.

96 BLM-GLO. http://www.glorecords.blm.gov/results/default.aspx? searchCriteria=type=patent|st=AL|cty=003|ln=mayo|fn=william|sp=true|sw=true| sadv=false (accessed: March 2014).

97 "Alabama, County Marriages, 1809-1950," index and images, *FamilySearch* (https://familysearch.org/pal:/MM9.1.1/XTWT-P5C : accessed 15 Mar 2014), Adam Brown and Eliza Sims, 16 May 1875; citing Baldwin County; FHL microfilm 1839621.

98 "Alabama, County Marriages, 1809-1950," index and images, *FamilySearch* (https://familysearch.org/pal:/MM9.1.1/XTWT-RZ3 : accessed 15 Mar 2014),

Brown married Victoria Saunders, 28 November, 1889, at Little River, Baldwin County. Rev. A. A. Williams officiated.[99] In the 1920 Census, the census taker incorrectly stated that Rev. Brown could not read or write. He was a farmer. He resided with wife, Victoria, daughter Ada Weeks, and grandchildren.[100]

Adam Brown and Nora Williams, 20 Dec 1884; citing Baldwin County; FHL microfilm 1839621.

99 "Alabama, County Marriages, 1809-1950," index and images, *FamilySearch* (https://familysearch.org/pal:/MM9.1.1/XTWY-SYR : accessed 15 Mar 2014), Adam Brown and Victoria Saunders, 28 Nov 1889; citing Baldwin County; FHL microfilm 1839622.

100 "United States Census, 1920," index and images, *FamilySearch* (https://familysearch.org/pal:/MM9.1.1/MXCL-YZM : accessed 19 Mar 2014), Adam Brown, Blackshear, Baldwin, Alabama, United States; citing sheet 5A, family 96, NARA microfilm publication T625, FHL microfilm 1820002.

1880
Baldwin County, Alabama

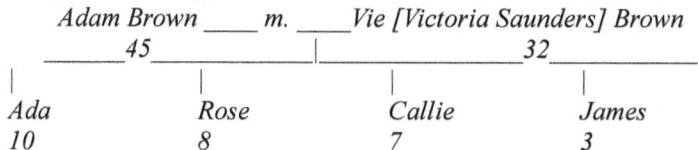

Adam Brown ____ m. ____*Vie [Victoria Saunders] Brown*
____45____|____32____

Ada	*Rose*	*Callie*	*James*
10	*8*	*7*	*3*

James Brown purchased land in Baldwin County, in 1903.[101]

101BLM-GLO. http://www.glorecords.blm.gov/results/default.aspx?
    searchCriteria=type=patent|st=AL|cty=003|ln=brown|sp=true|sw=true|sadv=false
    (accessed : March 2014).

Charles Daniels, J.P. N.P.

1811 -

Charles Daniels was born in 1811, in Alabama, resided with his family in Baldwin County, for the 1870 enumeration.[102] He married Elizabeth Davis, at night, in 1863, in Baldwin County.[103] U. B. *[Aubrey]* Philips, Minister of the Gospel, officiated. Occasionally crossing the color line to officiate at African-American weddings, Charles Daniels, Justice of the Peace, and Notary Public, officiated the marriage of Charles Kelson and Azilla Mack, his neighbors, at Monday Kelson's house, 12th January, 1882. Apparently, a double wedding, because the other couple, Lewis Williams and Emma Glassgo, were married that day. Justice Daniels was a person of color, because Rev. Phillips officiated at his wedding, and "Daniels" is a Native surname.[104]

102"United States Census, 1870," index and images, *FamilySearch* (https://familysearch.org/pal:/MM9.1.1/MHKH-QQ9 : accessed 13 Mar 2014), Charles Daniels, Alabama, United States; citing p. 4, family 25, NARA microfilm publication M593, FHL microfilm 000545500.

103"Alabama, County Marriages, 1809-1950," index and images, *FamilySearch* (https://familysearch.org/pal:/MM9.1.1/XTWT-LQF : accessed 13 Mar 2014), Charley Daniels and Elizabeth Davis, 22 Dec 1863; citing Baldwin County; FHL microfilm 1839621.

104AccessGenealogy.com. http://www.accessgenealogy.com/data/dawes.php? s_tribe=&s_last=daniels&s_first= (accessed: March 2014).

Table 4. Licensed Marriage Officiants

Baldwin County, Alabama[105]
1863 - 1900

Name	Church Affiliation	City	African or Native Descent?
Batchelor, Wm.C., M.G.	Spring Hill M.E. Baptist		
Bell, Joseph B., J.P.B.C.			
Bishop, Robert N., J.P., B.C.			
Bayert, A.W., J.P., B.C.	Baptist		
Bonner, George M., J.P. B.C. deceased 1867[106]			
Boone, G.W., Rev.			
Bracy, Stephen B., Rev.	Macedonia Missionary Baptist Church		Yes
Breton, L.C., N.P., J.P.			
Brown, Adam, M.G.			Yes
Bryars, John L., M.G.			Yes
Burke, Virgil, M.G., Elder	Zion Chapel Methodist		Yes
Byrne, D.C. J.P.		Bay Minette	

105"Alabama, County Marriages, 1809-1950," index and images, *FamilySearch* (accessed: March 2014).

106"Alabama, Estate Files, 1830-1976," index and images, *FamilySearch* (https://familysearch.org/pal:/MM9.1.1/VNTV-HPZ : accessed 16 Mar 2014), Geo M Bonner, 1867; citing Baldwin County County; FHL microfilm 2322454.

Name	Church Affiliation	City	African or Native Descent?
Carmichael, D.H., M.G.		Daphne	
Coleman, John C., M.G.			Yes
Collins, S.P., Minister			
Cooper, J.I., M.G.			
Daniels, Charles, N.P., J.P.			
Davis, Elvis, Pastor			
		Stockton	
Ellis, Jefferson, M.G.	**Bethel Baptist**	**Daphne**	**Yes**
Eslava, Joachim, J.P.M.C.		Mobile	
Feist, Adolph, J.P.			
Grace, John J., M.G.			
Gasgue, William H., Judge of Probate			
Graham, Elijah E., M.G.			
Graham, W.W., Minister			
Hall, C.H., J.P.			
Hall, O.P., Judge of Probate			
Hamilton, C.L.W., M.G.		Stockton	
Inge, Peter, M.G.			

Table 4. Licensed Marriage Officiants cont'd
Baldwin County, Alabama
1863 - 1900

Name	Church Affiliation	City	African or Native Descent?
Jackson, Ed, M.G.			Yes
Jacobs, John, M.G.			Yes
James, Joshua, Minister		Bay Minette	Yes
Jones, Alexis, M.G.			
Kelley, James M., J.P.			
Lambert, A.J., M.G.			
Leggett, Will, M.G.			Yes
Lewis, G.C., J.P. B.C.			
Maddox, D.W., M.G.			
Martin, P.L., Minister			
Mason, Wiley, M.G., Pastor Tate's Chapel AME		Daphne	Yes
Mayo, A., M.G.			Yes
Mayo, William D., P.E., Rev.			Yes
McCauley, Wm. H.,			
McConnell, R.D., J.P.		Bay Minette	
McConnell, Robt. L.M. N.P.*			
McCormick, Robt. L., N.P.			
McGowan, Thos. G., Rev.			
Mitchell, J.C., Rev.			
Monday, Henry, M.G.			Yes
Moore, Nelson, Gospel Min.		Mobile	
Nelson, Joseph, Elder			
Oldfield, Logan W., M.G.			Yes
Oliver, Lewis, M.G.			
Pace, John A., Minister		Mobile	
Pellicer, A.D., V.G., Pastor Mobile Cathedral		Mobile	
Phillips, U.B. [Aubrey], M.G.			Yes
Presley, Evans, J.P.			

---

*   Abbreviations: N.P. was Notary Public. M.G. was Minister of the Gospel. J.P. was Justice of the Peace. B.C. was Baldwin County.

Table 4. Licensed Marriage Officiants cont'd
Baldwin County, Alabama
1863 - 1900

Name	Church Affiliation	City	African or Native Descent?
Pughs, Jas. F., J.P.			
Raymond, Thos. H., M.G.		Mobile	
Richardson, R.R., J.P,		5th Precinct	
Robinson, Edward [Edmond], M.G.		Stockton	
Roy, S.R., J.P.			
Sansom, D.T., Rector	Christ Church	Mobile	
Sansom, Henry, Rector	Christ Church	Mobile	
Shadrick, Henderson, M.G.			
Shields, S.W., M.G.			
Simon, Hampton, M.G.		Mobile	Yes
Singleton, Thomas, M.G.	Baptist	Stockton	Yes
Singleton, William, M.G.	Baptist	Stockton	Yes
Spence, J.A., M.G.		Mobile	
Spratley, Ephraim, M.G.	Baptist		Yes
Stanley, Haywood, M.G.	Spring Hill Church	Tatemville Montrose	Yes
Stanford			
Sterling, M.G.	Bethel Baptist	Montrose	Yes
Thomas, Jesse B., J.P.			
Treadwell, J.E., Pastor			
Welch, J.H., M.G.	Methodist Church		
Wilkins, C.W., Judge of Probate			

Table 4. Licensed Marriage Officiants cont'd
Baldwin County, Alabama
1863 - 1900

Name	Church Affiliation	City	African or Native Descent?
Williams, Alfred A., M.G.	Macedonia Missionary Baptist	Daphne	Yes
	St. Joseph's Church		
Williams, Dan, N.P., B.C.	Baptist	Stockton	
Williams, Hank [sic], M.G.			Yes
Williams, Richard, M.G.		Mobile	Yes
Williams, Thomas, M.G.		Mobile	Yes
Wilson, John, N.P., J.P.			
Worden, John M., J.P.			

Table 5. Ministers of the Gospel

Baldwin County, Alabama
1863 - 1900

Name	Church Affiliation	City	African or Native Descent?
Batcheler, W.C., M.G.	Spring Hill M.E.		
Boone, G.W., Rev.			
Bracy, Stephen B., Rev.	Macedonia Missionary Baptist Church		Yes
Brown, Adam, M.G.			Yes
Bryars, J.L., M.G.			Native
Burke, Virgil,	M.G., Elder Zion Chapel		Yes
Carmichael, D.H., M.G.		Daphne	
Coleman, John C., M.G.			Yes
Collins, S.P., Minister			
Cooper, J.I., M.G.			
Davis, Elvis, Pastor		Stockton	
Ellis, Jefferson, M.G.	Bethel Baptist	Daphne	Yes
Grace, John J., M.G.			
Graham, Elijah E., M.G.			
Graham, W.W., Minister			
Hamilton, C.L.W., M.G.		Stockton	
Inge, Peter, M.G.			Yes
Jackson, Ed, M.G.			Yes
Jacobs, John, M.G.			Yes
James, Joshua, Minister		Bay Minette	Yes
Jones, Alexis, M.G.			

Table 5. Ministers of the Gospel cont'd
Baldwin County, Alabama
1863 - 1900

Name	Church Affiliation	City	African or Native Descent?
Lambert, A.J., M.G.			
Leggett, Will, M.G.			Yes
Maddox, D.W., M.G.			
Martin, P.L., Minister			
Mason,			
Wiley, M.G., Pastor	Tate's Chapel AME	Daphne	Yes
Mayo, A., M.G.			Yes
Mayo, William D., P.E., Rev.			Yes
McCauley, Wm. H.,			
McGowan, T.G., Rev.			
Mitchell, J.C., Rev.			
Monday, Henry, M.G.			Yes
Moore, Nelson, Gospel Min.		Mobile	Yes
Nelson, Joseph, Elder			
Oldfield, Logan W., M.G.			Yes
Oliver, Lewis, M.G.			
Pace, John A., Minister		Mobile	
Pellican, A.D., V.G., Pastor	Mobile Cathedral	Mobile	
Phillips, U.B., M.G.		Mobile	Yes
Raymond, Thos. H., M.G.		Mobile	Yes
Robinson, Edward, M.G.		Stockton	
Sansom, D.T., Rector	Christ Church	Mobile	
Sansom, Henry, Rector	Christ Church	Mobile	
Shadwick, Henderson, M.G.			Yes
Shields, S.W., M.G.			
Simon, Hampton, M.G.		Mobile	Yes
Singleton,			

Table 5. Ministers of the Gospel cont'd
Baldwin County, Alabama
1863 - 1900

Name	Church Affiliation	City	African or Native Descent?
Thomas, M.G. Baptist		Stockton	Yes
Singleton, William, M.G. Baptist		Stockton	Yes
Spence, J.A., M.G.		Mobile	
Spratley, Ephraim, M.G. Baptist			Yes
Stanley, Haywood, M.G.	Spring Hill Church	Tatemville Montrose	Yes
Stanford Sterling, M.G.	Bethel Baptist	Montrose	Yes
Treadwell, J.E., Pastor			
Welch, J.H., M.G.	Methodist Church		
Williams, Alfred A., M.G.	Macedonia Missionary Baptist	Daphne	Yes
	St. Joseph's Church		
Williams, H., M.G.			Yes
Williams, Richard, M.G.		Mobile	Yes
Williams, Thomas, M.G.			Yes

Table 6. Places of Interest - The Perfect Wedding Tour[107]

Sibley's Mill	*A.J. Carney's*
Carney's Still	*Fish River*
Schomo Plantation	*Holmes Plantation*
Zion Chapel	*Zion Church - Lewis Oliver, M.G.*

Judge's Office	*Courthouse*
Methodist Church	*Montrose*
Sims [sic] Hammock	*Greenwoods*
Fly Creek - Fairhope	*McCoy's Still*
at the Baptist Church	*W.M. Carney's*
Wolf Creek - Daphne	*the Village - present day Daphne*

McCoy & Sea's	*Mona [sic] Hammock*
Spring Hill Church	*F.J. McCoy's*
at Hudson Womack's House	*Atkinson's Hammock*
Montgomery Hill	*Roaring Branch*
Jack Springs	*Monday Kelson's - Montgomery Hill*

Battles Wharf	*Little River*
Dreisbach's	*Henry Monday's*
R. J. Moore's Hammock	*Little River*
Tenkey Branch	*Hammerville Distillery*
Tate's Chapel	*Dreisbach's Hammock*
at Rev. J. Ellis' House	*Steadham's Hammock*
	Silver Hill

107

"Alabama, County Marriages, 1809-1950," index and images, *FamilySearch* (*a*ccessed: March 2014).

Exhibit 2. Marriage Authorization

Baldwin County, Alabama

State of Alabama   )
*   )*
Baldwin County   )
*   )   To any Ordained*
or Licensed Minister, Judge of the Circuit, or Probate
Courts, or Justice of the Peace, for said County,
Greetings: You are hereby authorized to celebrate the
Rites of Matrimony between GROOM and BRIDE, and
this shall be your sufficient authority for so doing.
Given under my hand and seal, this DAY of MONTH,
YEAR.

Judge of Probate

The above named parties were married by me at
VENUE, on the DAY of MONTH, YEAR.

Title (Minister of the Gospel, Justice of the

Peace, etc.)

The Trustees of
BETHEL BAPTIST CHURCH
Daphne, Alabama

Plaque at Little Bethel Baptist Church
Daphne, Alabama

On April 15, 1867, Major Lewis Starke deeded
these two acres to ... and theirheirs as trustees for this church:
Nimrod Lovett,Stamford Starling (now Sterling), Narcis Elwa,
and Benjamin Franklin...[108]

Was Reverend Jeffrey Ellis buried in the church cemetery, in 1890?

Nimrod Lovett

1812 - before 1900

Nimrod Lovett, born in 1812, in North Carolina, (Alabama was not yet a state), married Hannah (unknown), resided in Baldwin County, in 1880, his only enumeration.[109] His name was struck on the census page. He suffered from paralysis. Lovitt *[Lovett]* voted in 1867, in Baldwin County.[110] Lovitt was one of four former slaves deeded land for the building of *[Little]* Bethel Baptist Church, in Daphne, Alabama, in 1867.[111]

108
   Ibid.
109"United States Census, 1880," index and images, *FamilySearch*
   (https://familysearch.org/pal:/MM9.1.1/M4N1-DRS : accessed 14 Mar 2014),
   Nimrod Lovitt, Court House, Baldwin, Alabama, United States; citing sheet
   198D, NARA microfilm publication T9.
110Alabama Department of Archives and History - ADAH.
   http://www.archives.alabama.gov/voterreg/results.cfm (accessed: March 2014).
111Baldwin County Churches.
   http://www.siteone.com/religion/baldwinchurches/index.html (accessed: March
   2014).

Genealogical Sources

1880
Baldwin County, Alabama

Nimrod Lovett _____ m. Hannah Lovett

_____

Stamford Starling [Stanford Sterling, M.G.]
aka Stamford Starke
1813 - 1898

Rev. Stanford Sterling, born in 1813, in North Carolina, (Alabama was not yet a state), resided with his wife, Piater *[Piety]* and children in Baldwin County, for the 1870 enumeration.[112] He was neighbor to Narciss Elva *[sic]* and Judge of Probate, Wm. H. Gasgue.[113] Stamford Starling *[sic]* married Piety Tripp, December 31, 1868, at Baldwin County.[114] His last enumeration was still in Baldwin County, with his family, in 1880.[115] Upon his death, February 5, 1898, his estate was probated at Baldwin County, Alabama.[116] His heirs were, Sandy Sterling, Isiah Sterling (resident of Mississippi), Mollie Ellis, his widow, Piety Sterling, and Judy Williams.[117] His widow, Piety Sterling was committed to an Insane Asylum.[118] Widow Sterling's stepson, Sandy S. Sterling received the house and two acres upon which it stood. Molly Sterling married Charles Ellis, at Greenwoods, Baldwin County, December 19, 1872. Reverend Jeffrey Ellis officiated.[119]

112"United States Census, 1870," index and images, *FamilySearch* (https://familysearch.org/pal:/MM9.1.1/MHK4-DLX : accessed 14 Mar 2014), Stanford Sterling, Alabama, United States; citing p. 13, family 123, NARA microfilm publication M593, FHL microfilm 000545500.
113Ibid.
114"Alabama, County Marriages, 1809-1950," index and images, *FamilySearch* (https://familysearch.org/pal:/MM9.3.1/TH-1-9819-71564-60?cc=1743384 : accessed 14 Mar 2014), 1839621 (004539243) > image 635 of 1059.
115"United States Census, 1880," index and images, *FamilySearch* (https://familysearch.org/pal:/MM9.1.1/M4N1-DRJ : accessed 14 Mar 2014), Standford Sterling, Court House, Baldwin, Alabama, United States; citing sheet 198D, NARA microfilm publication T9.
116"Alabama, Estate Files, 1830-1976," index and images, *FamilySearch* (https://familysearch.org/pal:/MM9.3.1/TH-1951-23277-11893-37?cc=1978117 : accessed 14 Mar 2014), Baldwin > Sterling, Stanford (1898) > image 4 of 20.
117Ibid.
118Ibid.
119"Alabama, County Marriages, 1809-1950," index and images, *FamilySearch* (https://familysearch.org/pal:/MM9.3.1/TH-1-9819-70553-11?cc=1743384 : accessed 14 Mar 2014), 1839621 (004539243) > image 676 of 1059.

1870
Baldwin County, Alabama

Standford Sterling _____ m. _____Piety Tripp Sterling

Narciss Eliva [Elwa]

1824 - before 1880

Narciss Elwa, born 1824, in Alabama, resided with his wife Dolly, in Baldwin County, for the 1870 enumeration.[120] His son lived but doors away.[121] His daughter, Cora Elwa, married Washington Evans, November 15, 1868, in Baldwin County, at Bethel Baptist Church. Rev. Jefferson Ellis officiated.[122]

Benjamin Franklin

1804 - before 1900

Benjamin Franklin, born 1804, in Georgia, resided with his wife Maria, and children, were neighbors to the Sterlings, in Baldwin County, for the 1880 enumeration.[123] His only other enumeration was

---

120"United States Census, 1870," index and images, *FamilySearch* (https://familysearch.org/pal:/MM9.3.1/TH-266-13035-8510-61?cc=1438024 : accessed 14 Mar 2014), Alabama > Baldwin > Township 5 > image 13 of 16; citing NARA microfilm publication M593.

121Ibid.

122"Alabama, County Marriages, 1809-1950," : accessed 14 Mar 2014), 1839621 (004539243) > image 633 of 1059.

123"United States Census, 1880," index and images, *FamilySearch* (https://familysearch.org/pal:/MM9.1.1/M4N1-DRL : accessed 14 Mar 2014), Benj Franklin, Court House, Baldwin, Alabama, United States; citing sheet 198D, NARA microfilm publication T9.

in 1866, for Baldwin County, Alabama.[124] He voted in 1867.[125] His descendant, Ben Franklin married Massey Alexander, July 9, 1891, Baldwin County, Judge Gasgue officiated.[126] Rev. Ellis died in 1890.

124"Alabama, State Census, 1866," index, *FamilySearch*
(https://familysearch.org/pal:/MM9.1.1/V6PL-VH7 : accessed 14 Mar 2014),
Benjamin Franklin, Baldwin, Alabama; citing Department of Archives and
History, Montgomery; FHL microfilm 1533830.
125ADAH.
126"Alabama, County Marriages, 1809-1950," index and images, *FamilySearch*
(https://familysearch.org/pal:/MM9.1.1/XTWY-36P : accessed 14 Mar 2014),
Ben Franklin and Massey Alexander, 09 Jul 1891; citing Baldwin County; FHL
microfilm 1839622.

Table 7. Affiliated Churches in Baldwin County, Alabama

*[Little] Bethel Baptist Church
at Montrose [Daphne]
1867*

*[Little] Zion United Methodist Church
at Tensaw*

*Macedonia Missionary Baptist Church
at Daphne
1867*

*Colored [African] Methodist Episcopal Church
at Montrose
1867*

*[First Baptist] Church Silverhill
at Silverhill*

*Tate Chapel [AME Church]
at Little River*

St. Joseph's Church

****

*Spring Hill Methodist Episcopal Church
at Mobile
1874*

BLACK CHURCH.

Black Church. *Courtesy of the New York Public Library, Digital Collections.*

John C. Coleman, M.G.

1819 - before 1880

John C. Coleman, M.G., voted in 1867, in Baldwin County.[127] He was born in 1819, in Alabama, and enumerated in the household of William Poter, in 1870.[128] He could neither read nor write, and worked as a farm hand.[129] 1870 was his only enumeration.

Will Leggett, M.G.

1872 - 1951

Willie *[sic]* Legget, born in 1872, in Alabama, resided with his family in Baldwin County, for the 1880 enumeration.[130] His parents were Samuel and Ary, and he was the young neighbor of Rev. Spratley.[131] In 1910, he resided at Blacksher, Baldwin County, with his mother Aarie *[sic]*, and wife, Elossie.[132] Clarissa York married Willie Legget, in 1910, in Baldwin County.[133] Rev. C. Luciano officiated, at Tensaw, Baldwin County, Alabama.[134] Clarissa Baker Leggett, died in

---

127ADAH, Coleman.
128"United States Census, 1870," John Coleman in household of William Poter, Alabama, United States; citing p. 8, family 59, NARA microfilm publication M593, FHL microfilm 000545500.
129Ibid.
130"United States Census, 1880," index and images, *FamilySearch* (https://familysearch.org/pal:/MM9.1.1/M4N1-WMV : accessed 25 Mar 2014), Willie Leggett in household of Saml Leggett, Montgomery Hill, Baldwin, Alabama, United States; citing sheet 153A, NARA microfilm publication T9.
131Ibid.
132"United States Census, 1910," index and images, *FamilySearch* (https://familysearch.org/pal:/MM9.1.1/MK3V-H6H : accessed 25 Mar 2014), Willie Leggett, Blacksher, Baldwin, Alabama, United States; citing enumeration district (ED) 1, sheet 13A, family 187, NARA microfilm publication T624, FHL microfilm 1374014.
133"Alabama, County Marriages, 1809-1950," : accessed 23 Mar 2014), Willie Leggett and Clarissa York, 07 Mar 1910; citing Baldwin County; FHL microfilm 1839624.
134Ibid.

1940 at Baldwin County, Alabama.[135] Rev. Will Leggett died at
Baldwin County, in 1951.[136]

Hampton Simon, M.G.

1829 - before 1900

Hampton Simon, M.G., was born in 1829, in Alabama, was literate,
and resided with his wife, Martha, at Mount Vernon, Mobile County,
for the 1880 enumeration.[137] He probably voted in 1867, but the name
listed was "Haywood.[138]" He married Martha Williams, in 1880, in
Mobile.[139]   He was not found further in the record. Reverend Simon,
was most identified with Mobile.

Virgil Burke, M.G.

1800 - before 1900

Virgil Burke, M.G., was born in North Carolina, in 1800, was literate,
and resided with his wife, Phoebe *[sic]*, in Mobile County, for the
1870 enumeration.[140] Rev. Burke identified himself as a "Methodist

135"Alabama, Deaths, 1908-1974," index, *FamilySearch*
    (https://familysearch.org/pal:/MM9.1.1/JDYB-PTS : accessed 23 Mar 2014),
    Clarissa Legett, 14 Jun 1940; citing reference cn 13049, Department of Health,
    Montgomery; FHL microfilm 1908589.
136"Alabama, Deaths, 1908-1974," : accessed 25 Mar 2014), Willie Leggett, 29
    Nov 1951; citing reference 22005, Department of Health, Montgomery; FHL
    microfilm 1908863.
137"United States Census, 1880," index and images, *FamilySearch*
    (https://familysearch.org/pal:/MM9.1.1/M4V3-HLQ : accessed 22 Mar 2014),
    Hampton Simon, Mount Vernon, Mobile, Alabama, United States; citing sheet
    23A, NARA microfilm publication T9.
138ADAH - Simon, Mobile.
139"Alabama, County Marriages, 1809-1950," index and images, *FamilySearch*
    (https://familysearch.org/pal:/MM9.1.1/VRVM-W2F : accessed 22 Mar 2014),
    Hampton Simon and Martha Williams, 05 Feb 1880; citing Mobile County; FHL
    microfilm 1294438.
140"United States Census, 1870," index and images, *FamilySearch*

Preacher," in the 1880 Census.[141] He resided with his wife, Phoebe, and granddaughter, Mary Downeal.[142]

Rev. Burke was most identified with Zion Chapel, and Mobile.

William C. Batcheler [Bachelor], M.G.

1811 - before 1880

William Bachelor's wife, Missouri Lee Bachelor, died at Stockton, Baldwin County, Alabama, in 1929.[143] Wm. Bachelor *[sic]* married Missouri Lee, in 1920, in Baldwin County. Rev. Wm. Ricks officiated.[144] He was not the Reverend Batchelor, because he was too young.

Willie Batchler *[sic]* married Annetta Heill, in Mobile, in 1905, Colored Book No. 17 Pg. 341.[145] Willie Batcheller *[sic]*, resided with his family at Stockton and Deans, Baldwin County, for the 1910 enumeration.[146] He was not the Reverend Batchelor, because he was

---

(https://familysearch.org/pal:/MM9.1.1/MHKL-7X8 : accessed 22 Mar 2014), Virgil Burke, Alabama, United States; citing p. 52, family 334, NARA microfilm publication M593, FHL microfilm 000545530.

141"United States Census, 1880," index and images, *FamilySearch* (https://familysearch.org/pal:/MM9.1.1/M4VQ-HQK : accessed 22 Mar 2014), Virgil Burke, Mobile, Mobile, Alabama, United States; citing sheet 282B, NARA microfilm publication T9.

142*Ibid.*

143"Alabama, Deaths, 1908-1974," index, *FamilySearch* (https://familysearch.org/pal:/MM9.1.1/JDNQ-8J5 : accessed 22 Mar 2014), Wm. Bachelor in entry for Missouri Bachelor, 23 Feb 1929; citing reference cn 4529, Department of Health, Montgomery; FHL microfilm 1908463.

144"Alabama, County Marriages, 1809-1950," index and images, *FamilySearch* (https://familysearch.org/pal:/MM9.1.1/XTW8-421 : accessed 22 Mar 2014), W H Bachelder and Missouri Lee, 11 Dec 1920; citing Baldwin County; FHL microfilm 1839624.

145"Alabama, County Marriages, 1809-1950," index and images, *FamilySearch* (https://familysearch.org/pal:/MM9.1.1/VRVM-1J8 : accessed 22 Mar 2014), Willie Batchler and Annetta Heill, 30 Mar 1905; citing Mobile County; FHL microfilm 1294441.

146"United States Census, 1910," index and images, *FamilySearch* (https://familysearch.org/pal:/MM9.1.1/MK3V-8R8 : accessed 22 Mar 2014),

too young.

Wm. C. Batchelor, born in 1811, in England, resided with his family in Baldwin County, for the 1870 enumeration.[147] Rev. Hayward *[sic]* Stanley lived nearby. Son, Wm. Batchelor, born 1839, in Missouri, married, boarded in the household of Wm. Weekley, Baldwin County, for the 1880 enumeration.[148]

Rev. William C. Batchelor, was most identified with Spring Hill M.E. Church and Stockton, Baldwin County, Alabama.

Peter Inge, M.G.

1837 - before 1900

Peter Inge, M.G., was born in 1837, in Alabama, resided with his wife, Louisa, for the 1870 enumeration, in Mobile.[149]   Peter Inge voted in 1867.[150] Peter Inge married Louisa Harper, in Mobile, in 1873.[151] In the 1880 Census, Mobile County, Rev. Inge was literate.[152] Reverend

Willie Batcheller, Stockton and Deans, Baldwin, Alabama, United States; citing enumeration district (ED) 3, sheet 7A, family 118, NARA microfilm publication T624, FHL microfilm 1374014.

147"United States Census, 1870," index and images, *FamilySearch* (https://familysearch.org/pal:/MM9.1.1/MHKH-83J : accessed 22 Mar 2014), Wm C Batchelor, Alabama, United States; citing p. 4, family 28, NARA microfilm publication M593, FHL microfilm 000545500.

148"United States Census, 1880," index and images, *FamilySearch* (https://familysearch.org/pal:/MM9.1.1/M4N1-WBF : accessed 22 Mar 2014), Wm Batchelor in household of Wm Weekley, Montgomery Hill, Baldwin, Alabama, United States; citing sheet 140D, NARA microfilm publication T9.

149"United States Census, 1870," index and images, *FamilySearch* (https://familysearch.org/pal:/MM9.1.1/MHK2-TC1 : accessed 23 Mar 2014), Peter Inge, Alabama, United States; citing p. 89, family 635, NARA microfilm publication M593, FHL microfilm 000545530.

150ADAH - Inge.

151"Alabama, County Marriages, 1809-1950," index and images, *FamilySearch* (https://familysearch.org/pal:/MM9.1.1/VRVS-T5L : accessed 23 Mar 2014), Peter Inge and Louisa Harper, 04 Jun 1873; citing Mobile County; FHL microfilm 1294441.

152"United States Census, 1880," index and images, *FamilySearch* (https://familysearch.org/pal:/MM9.1.1/M4VQ-TCS : accessed 23 Mar 2014),

Peter Inge was not found further in the record.

U. B. [Aubrey] Phillips, M.G.
1827 - before 1880

Rev. Aubrey Phillips was born in 1827, in Florida, and resided in the household of Polly Mitchell, in 1870.[153] Aubrey Phillips voted in 1867.[154] Rev. Phillips was not found further in the record. Rev. Phillips officiated at Charles Daniels wedding.

Thomas H. Raymond, M.G.
1826 -

Thomas H. Raymond voted in Mobile County, in 1867.[155] Thomas Raymond was a literate cotton sampler, in Mobile, for the 1870 enumeration.[156] Rev. Raymond was a native son of Alabama, born in 1826.[157] Rev. Raymond was not found further in the record.

J. A. Spence, M.G.
unknown - before 1900

Josh Spence was listed on the death record of his daughter, Tempe

---

Peter Inge, Mobile, Mobile, Alabama, United States; citing sheet 431C, NARA microfilm publication T9.

153"United States Census, 1870," index and images, *FamilySearch* (https://familysearch.org/pal:/MM9.1.1/MHK2-1WW : accessed 23 Mar 2014), Aubrey Phillips in household of Polly Mitchell, Alabama, United States; citing p. 43, family 353, NARA microfilm publication M593, FHL microfilm 000545530.

154ADAH - Phillips.

155ADAH - Raymond.

156"United States Census, 1870," Thos Raymond, Alabama, United States; citing p. 57, family 371, NARA microfilm publication M593, FHL microfilm 000545530.

157Ibid.

Ganey, in 1924, in Baldwin County.[158] Her internment was at the Methodist Episcopal Church Cemetery, in Lottie, Baldwin County.[159] Joshua Spence signed the marriage bond for daughter, Nancy, in 1897, in Baldwin County.[160] Joshua Spence was not found further in the record. Based on the meager evidence, Rev. J. A. Spence was not a man of color.

Nelson Moore, M.G.

1835 - before 1900

Rev. Nelson Moore was born in 1835, in Alabama, and resided in Mobile, Mobile County, Alabama, for the 1866 enumeration.[161] Nelson Moore was enumerated in 1870, with his wife, Lizzie, and family. He was an engineer.[162] Rev. Moore was enumerated in 1880, in Mobile, as a Methodist minister, with his wife Elizabeth, and servant, Caroline Aaron.[163]

1870
Mobile County, Alabama

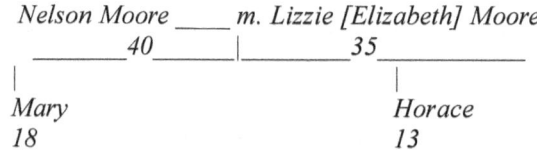

```
Nelson Moore _____ m. Lizzie [Elizabeth] Moore
_____40_____|_____35_____
|                        |
Mary                     Horace
18                       13
```

158"Alabama, Deaths, 1908-1974," Josh Spence in entry for Tempy Ganey, 28 Jan 1924; citing reference cn 2243, Department of Health, Montgomery; FHL microfilm 1908256.

159Ibid.

160"Alabama, County Marriages, 1809-1950," Hossie E Presley and Nancy Spence, 16 Dec 1897; citing Baldwin County; FHL microfilm 1839624.

161"United States Census, 1880," Peter Inge, Mobile, Mobile, Alabama, United States; citing sheet 431C, NARA microfilm publication T9.

162"United States Census, 1870," Nelson Moore in household of Lizzie Moore, Alabama, United States; citing p. 109, family 839, NARA microfilm publication M593, FHL microfilm 000545530.

163"United States Census, 1880," Nelson More, Manvilla, Mobile, Alabama, United States; citing sheet 51A, NARA microfilm publication T9.

Adam Mayo, M.G.

1817 -

Reverend Adam Mayo, was born in 1817, in Tennessee. He lived alone, for the 1870 enumeration, in Beat 1, Monroe County, Alabama.[164] The census taker noted idiotically, that he could read but not write, and was either deaf, dumb, idiotic, blind, or insane.[165] 1870 was Rev. Mayo's only enumeration.

164"United States Census, 1870," Adam Mayo, Alabama, United States; citing p. 8, family 58, NARA microfilm publication M593, FHL microfilm 000545531.
165Ibid.

C o n c l u s i o n

Through a genealogical approach, we have sought to undergird the historical record, specifically the underpinnings of African-American history during Reconstruction. This approach satisfactorily enabled historical excavation of previously neglected men of the cloth. Names, places, and motives were unearth. The genealogical approach provided a prosthetic for amputated documentary evidence. Based on the work of Elizabeth Shown-Mills,[166] our initial case in point, Jefferson Ellis, Minister of the Gospel, we learned that he was intertwined with family, numerous wedding couples, fellow ministers, and community leaders. By following his associations, we uncovered some facets of the man, his mission, and his motives. By extension, we were able to project a range encompassing other members of his religious and civic umbrella, identifying more than two dozen men of color, in the service of their respective churches and affiliations. That ministerial network is worth recognizing for now, and into the future.

Patterns and practices evolved over time, and were evident in the record. Those practices entailed the revolutionary concept of accommodating black ministers for marriages. This practice, mandated by Alabama's assistant commissioner, to the Freedmens Bureau, in 1865, was groundbreaking. However, noticeably absent from the licensing record were instances of men of color holding civil office, such as justices, notaries public, or Judge of Probate. However, on closer inspection, we found that men like Charles W. Wilkins, Judge of Probate, was, likely a "man of color." And, Charles Daniels, J.P., too, was a free person of color. Both men were of Creek descent. In 1866, the volume of couples applying for licenses exceeded the supply of officiants. In 1867, Jefferson Ellis, M.G.

166Elizabeth Shown-Mills, The Historical Biographer's Guide to Cluster Research (the FAN Principle).

made his first appearance in the record. He was later joined by Haywood Stanley, M.G., and William D. Mayo, M.G. They were the first tier of ministers of color. The genealogical record evinced in the marriage records, provided clear evidence that the second tier of ministers were recruited, mentored, and sponsored by Reverends Ellis, Stanley, Alfred A. Williams, and Mayo. Ephraim Spratley, Stephen B. Bracy, and others, continued their minitries. Contrary to stereotype, nearly all of these men were literate, and members of the second tier were able to dedicate themselves solely to their vocation.

Between 1867 and 1874, several notable black churches were formed: *[Little]* Bethel Baptist, Macedonia Missionary Baptist, Colored *[African]* Methodist Episcopal, at Montrose, and Tate's Chapel *[AME]*, at Little River, to name a few.

Supplementing historical documentary evidence with a genealogical approach has clarified as well as amplified the historical record. Parsing historical documents yielded names and places, a genealogical technique that illuminated the statistical and ethnic makeup of those whose names and places resounded for descendants and others, seeking to peek behind the curtain.

©2014 - 2016

[18] "Alabama, County Marriages, 1809-1950", database with images, *FamilySearch* (https://familysearch.org/ark:/61903/1:1:XTWT-R8X : accessed 9 June 2016), Henry J Smith and Fannie Gentry, 1866.

[19] Library of Congress, "A Century of Lawmaking for a New Nation: U.S. Congressional Documents and Debates, 1774 - 1875," *American State Papers, House of Representatives, 14th Congress, 1st Session, Public Lands: Volume 3, page 15, Claims East of Pearl River, James Ellis, No. 47.http://memory.loc.gov/cgi-bin/ampage*

[20] "United States Census, 1860", database with images, *FamilySearch* (https://familysearch.org/ark:/61903/1:1:MHD4-LKF : accessed 9 June 2016), Lowry Ellis, 1860.

[21] GenealogyBank.com, by Telegraph from Washington, http://genealogybank.com/gbnk/newspapers/doc/v2:10EEA65... (accessed: March 2014).

[22] Ibid.

[23] Elizabeth Shown-Mills, The Historical Biographer's Guide to Cluster Research (the FAN Principle), (Baltimore: Genealogical Publishing Co., 2009) ISBN 978-0-8063-1894-3.

[24] BLM, Bureau of Land Management. http://www.glorecords.blm.gov/search/default.aspx#searchTabIndex=0&searchByTypeIndex=0 (accessed : March 2014).

[25] The Encyclopedia of Alabama. http://www.encyclopediaofalabama.org/face/Article.jsp?id=h-3137. Turpentine Industry in Alabama, (accessed : March 2014).

[26] "Alabama, Deaths, 1908-1974," index, *FamilySearch* (https://familysearch.org/pal:/MM9.1.1/JDLB-SXR : accessed 09 Mar 2014), Jeffrey Ellis in entry for Cornelia Bailey, 24 Mar 1930; citing reference cn 4879, Department of Health, Montgomery; FHL microfilm 1908475.

[27] "Alabama, County Marriages, 1809-1950," Jeffery Ellis Sarr [Sen.] and Ednny Lyons, 06 Nov 1876; citing Baldwin County; FHL microfilm 1839621.

[28] "United States Census, 1870," index and images, *FamilySearch* (https://familysearch.org/pal:/MM9.1.1/MHK4-R12 : accessed 17 Mar 2014), Edney Lions in household of Mike Lions, Alabama, United States; citing p. 9, family 80, NARA microfilm publication M593, FHL microfilm 000545500.

[29] "United States Census, 1880," index and images, *FamilySearch* (https://familysearch.org/pal:/MM9.1.1/M4N1-DHM : accessed 09 Mar 2014), Jeffrey Elles in household of William Bayley, Court House, Baldwin, Alabama, United States; citing sheet 193B, family 4, NARA microfilm publication T9-0001

[30] "Alabama, County Marriages, 1809-1950," index and images, *FamilySearch* (https://familysearch.org/pal:/MM9.1.1/XTWT-PTP : accessed 20 February 2015), Jeffrey Ellis and Lizzie White, 20 Jul 1880; citing Baldwin, Alabama, United States, county courthouses, Alabama; FHL microfilm 1,839,621.

[31] "Alabama, County Marriages, 1809-1950," : accessed 09 Mar 2014), Jeffery Ellis and Fannie Gardner, 1884.

32 http://exhibits.hsl.virginia.edu/yellowfever/ (accessed: March 2014).
33 Ibid., Image 606 of 1059.
34 Ibid.
35 "Alabama, County Marriages, 1809-1950," : accessed 10 Mar 2014),
    Anthony Ellis and Narcissa Mitchell, 1874.
36 Alabama Department of Archives and History - ADAH.
    http://www.archives.alabama.gov/voterreg/results.cfm, Ellis, Jefferson,
    (accessed: March 2014).
37 "United States Census, 1850," index and images, *FamilySearch*
    (https://familysearch.org/pal:/MM9.1.1/MHPR-ZN5 : accessed 20 February
    2015), Jefferson Ellis in household of Geo W Tucker, Bibb county, Bibb,
    Alabama, United States; citing family 652, NARA microfilm publication
    M432 (Washington, D.C.: National Archives and Records Administration,
    n.d.).
38 The Digital Library on American Slavery,
    http://library.uncg.edu/slavery/details.aspx?pid=10342 (accessed: March
    2014).
39 "United States Census, 1870," : accessed 10 Mar 2014), Lemuel Ellis,
    Alabama, United States; citing p. , family 735, NARA microfilm
    publication M593, FHL microfilm 000545530.
40 Bureau of Land Management,
    http://www.glorecords.blm.gov/results/default.aspx?
    searchCriteria=type=patent|st=AL|cty=003|ln=ellis|sp=true|sw=true|
    sadv=false (accessed: March 2014).
41 "Alabama, County Marriages, 1809-1950," : accessed 10 Mar 2014),
    Wellington Stendley and Agerrs Ellis, 1874. "Alabama, County Marriages,
    1809-1950," index and images, *FamilySearch*
    (https://familysearch.org/pal:/MM9.1.1/XTWT-G5T : accessed 27 Mar
    2014), Oliver Dumas and Alice Brown, 25 Nov 1874; citing Baldwin
    County; FHL microfilm 1839621.
42 Year: *1880*; Census Place: *Selma, Dallas, Alabama*; Roll: *11*; Family
    History Film: *1254011*; Page: *502D*; Enumeration District: *074*; Image:
    0778.
43 "Alabama, County Marriages, 1809-1950," James Henry Brown and Alice
    Ellis, 1871.
44 "Alabama, County Marriages, 1809-1950," Oliver Dumas and Alice
    Brown, 25 Nov 1874; citing Baldwin County; FHL microfilm 1839621.
45 "United States Census, 1880," Alice Dumas in household of Oliver Dumas,
    Court House, Baldwin, Alabama, United States; citing sheet 194D, NARA
    microfilm publication T9.
46 "Alabama, County Marriages, 1809-1950," Jeffrey Ellis and Lizzie White,
    1880.
47 "Alabama, County Marriages, 1809-1950," William Winesow [Winslow
    Bailey] and Cornelia Ellis, 1876.
48 "Alabama, County Marriages, 1809-1950," Andrew Ellis and Ellen
    Gardner, 1883.
49 "Alabama, Deaths, 1908-1974", Jeffrey Ellis in entry for Cornelia Bailey,
    24 Mar 1930.
50 "Alabama, County Marriages, 1809-1950," Henderson Ellis in entry for

John Hurley Ellis and Robie Pearl Greer, 1944.

[51] "Alabama, County Marriages, 1809-1950", Hamilton E Ellis and Minnie Eva Stafford, 1911.

[52] "United States Census, 1880", : accessed 10 Mar 2014), Jeffrey Ellis, 1880

[53] "Alabama, County Marriages, 1809-1950", T I Ellis and Pricilla Webster, 1877.

[54] "Alabama, County Marriages, 1809-1950", T J Ellis in entry for Thomas Ellis and Mary Williams, 1897.

[55] "United States Census, 1870", : accessed 12 Mar 2014), Hayward Stanley, 1870.

Alphabetical Index